JOE BIANCO

TREASURES ITALIAN:

Undiscovered

Sights & Tastes

of

Northern Italy

Avellino Press

Acknowledgments

When I returned home from a brief vacation visit to Mexico I had waiting for me a letter of invitation from Silverio Nardone of the Italian Government Tourist Board inviting me and a select group of journalists from throughout the U.S. to tour parts of northern Italy. The purpose of the trip was to better familiarize us with the lesser-known art cities in two of the most beautiful regions of Italy. It was the beginning of one of the most interesting journeys to the land of my ancestors. In this book I hope that my experiences during this journey can introduce a region of Italy that is often bypassed by less fortunate travelers.

I want to thank the Italian Government Tourist Board, its western USA director Silverio Nardone, the board's press representative Azita Nostrati, and Alitalia airlines and its representative, Marta Lotti, for making this trip possible. In addition, I want to thank my traveling colleagues for their companionship and harmony during the long hours of our enjoyable but work-filled days and nights. They were Jack Adler, bureau chief of *Travel Trade* and writer of Prodigy Internet; Richard Stayton, managing editor of *Westways* magazine; Michael Ardizzone, editor, *Travel Weekly Magazine*; Steve Bergsman, editor, *Travel Agent Magazine*; Anne Z. Cooke and Ellen Klugman, both nationally known travel writers; Eric Gutierrez, editor, *Genre Magazine*, and, last but not least, Armond Noble, publisher of *International Travel News*.

Thanks to Carlo Mannocci and Barbara Elder for assistance in translations.

A special thanks to Peggy for your patience and love.

Photography: Joe Bianco

Publication design & editing: Mary Margaret Hite

ISBN 0-9643408-5-2

Printed in the United States of America

05/05/02

Connie
Some good
recipes in here!
Hope you like them
of the book
Love,
Gloria

Table
of
Contents

Cover Photos

Front cover: Palazzo Te, Mantova
Back cover (clockwise from top left):
Cheesemaker Danilo Allegri at a dairy cooperative near
Parma; one of the many magnificent medieval cathe-
drals in Cremona; steamed salmon with courgettes, as
served in the Canova restaurant in Parma; elegant
service at Silverio Ristorante, Bologna; the 125, first
Ferrari built, at Galleria Ferrari classic car museum in
Maranello, near Modena

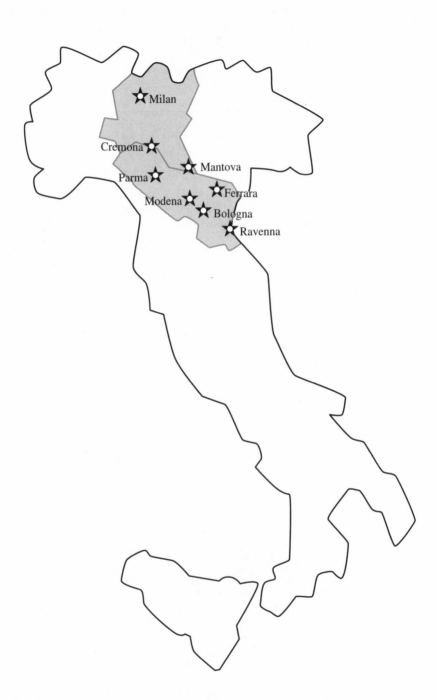

INTRODUCTION

As the huge Alitalia MD-11 landed softly at Milano's Malprensa airport, the journey to the land of the gourmet and traveler was truly beginning. What a joy to emerge from weeks of rain and wintry-like weather and find the clouds gone, the wet spring behind and the sun no longer in hiding! After the April rains and dark days of a sodden Portland and a misty Oregon, I arrived in the land of my forefathers where the weather is not frequently a topic of conversation and the word "sunny" is more often heard by the foreign traveler.

I was here with eight other colleague journalists to embark on a journey. Our mission was to explore the little-known art cities in the agriculturally rich Po Valley of the regions of Emilia-Romagna and Lombardy. Our first stop was to be Cremona, where Stradivari brought his genius, then on to Bologna where the culinary talents are unsurpassed. Next we would go to Modena, where the trebbiano grapes turned a vineyard into a treasure for the lovers who savor a balsamic flavor to their cuisine, and from there to Parma where prosciutto and cheese reign, finally to Ravenna, not to overlook the tomb of Dante, and to Mantova and other centers of art and food that make the Po so envied. Our guides were representatives of the Italian government tourist board and Alitalia air lines.

Here in Italy sophisticated hotels, grand theaters and opera houses, public gardens of grandiose design, impressive statues of historical design, elegant women and impeccably attired men are commonplace. Such attributes do not alter the warm and gracious attitude of the people of Italy, who lead the world in fashion and food.

I was flattered to be a descendant of the history and

culture of this wonderfully endowed country. Now, ahead was an adventure...the art and grandeur of the past and the present nation of 60 million souls enriched with history and living within the comfort of the fifth largest economy in the world.

Malprensa is one of two airports serving Italy's fashion capital and was extraordinarily quiet and smaller in comparison to Rome's Leonardo da Vinci airport at Fiumicino. The weather was ideal, a gift from nature that endured until our departure seven days later.

Representatives from the nearby city of Cremona, our first stop, greeted us with all the cordiality and respect one would expect to be extended to visiting dignitaries—not to journalists touting the wares of their trade.

Amanda Mazzucchi, one of the guides and translators, was very cordial. Her delightful stature and soft Cremonian voice enhanced the romantic qualities of my native English. She was equally conversant in French, the second and third language of many Italians in the north. Her companion guide, Lucia Bertolotti Quaini, was taller and her presence, knowledge and personality, too, only made the moments in Cremona ever more memorable.

We set off from Malprensa as the early afternoon sun began its westerly sweep of the northern plains of the Po Valley. In the distance, I could see the faint silhouette of the Alps to the north marking our entrance to this perpetually abundant countryside.

We traveled through enormous farms run by wealthy landowners or cooperatives and clearly there for centuries. Here and there as we motored in our Ziliani tour bus toward Cremona, our first stop, the cultivated land became more and more like my own Willamette Valley in Oregon, green and more green as far as the eye could see. We were entering the heart of the legendary Po Valley, famed for its rich and bountiful red hard winter durum wheat and its variety of other field and row crops. Here, too, the land yields the feed for the succulent pigs from which come the finest and tastiest hams in the world. Not to be overlooked, of course, is another famous product of this valley, parmesan cheese from Parma, only a short drive to the south from Cremona.

I remember reading about the Po Valley during my high school days and it fascinated me, because my youth was spent in the urban cities of the northeast: New York, Newark, Jersey City. I never thought one day I would see and travel in one of the most famous farmlands of Europe, and as a guest of the country, the native land of my parents.

This is truly the breadbasket of Italy. And there would be more definitely ahead for we were just beginning to savor this remarkable valley of the Po River. I was prepared as were my colleagues to cast aside all culinary restrictions and enjoy the feast of food which I'm sure was being planned for us in true Italian style. As my mother used to say, "the best way to make lasting friends is through the generosity of your kitchen."

What more can you ask for? As a writer and cook I was still searching for the culinary secrets of the Po, hoping they would be revealed to me. My mission here was to tap into the grandeur of the kitchens of Bologna, the culinary capital of Italy, which lies east of the northern Appenine range and west of the seacoast resorts of the upper Adriatic Sea. I was hoping for success even though our trip here was limited to only seven days...just seven days in Italy.

The imposing entrance to
Il Palazzo Communale, Cremona

We arrived at our hotel, on a small hillside on the edge of the city of Cremona, with just enough time to recapture some of our energy, change clothes and look somewhat alert for our meeting with the city's mayor and other dignitaries. It was late afternoon here, but early morning at home. We had lost part of a day during the eleven-hour flight from Los Angeles but would regain it, we had been promised, on our return flight.

The first stop for us was the municipal palace, Il Palazzo Comunale, which dates back several centuries to the time before an Italian explorer named Columbus changed the shape of the world.

Here, as I'm sure is elsewhere, the past is so intensively *present* that one wonders how the people can remain so enthusiastic about their history and yet escape the blasé attitude which normally affects those so richly endowed.

This medieval structure, a beautiful example of Lombard civil architecture, with a wide Gothic arcade underneath, remains substantially unaltered, I'm told, from the 15th Century. Further architectural reshaping was done later in the next century and the present-day arrangement of the façade was made in the early 1800s. Significant and careful refinishing continues not only in this palace but in many of the medieval buildings on our itinerary, for in Italy the past is preserved into the present for all to enjoy and to learn from.

We were escorted inside the palace to an upstairs reception room large enough to house a two-story dwelling and alive with the history of renaissance art adorning its walls. Here was a tall, thin, Lincolnesque figure of a man, and as he approached to welcome us his entourage faded to the rear of the enormous medieval room, affording him generous space for his welcoming remarks. This was the mayor, and our encounter with the first host of our visit.

Mayor Paolo Bodini, the "Sindaco," made his remarks brief:

"Your schedule is very tight, there is no question about it. I think you will find some interesting things in this area and carry back with you a good impression and a souvenir of your visit here.

"I hope the that the sound of the violin that you are about to enjoy...will sort of go deep into your soul and that you will take this 'souvenir' with you when you go back to the States."

No sooner had he finished speaking than suddenly a sweet sound came into the room, one that only can come from a violin. But this was not an ordinary violin, but rather one crafted by the town's most famous craftsman, Antonio Stradavari, in 1715.

It was a interlude that was impressive not so much because the violin was a rare object of art, but because the music offered a much-needed pause after such a long trip.

Afterwards the mayor invited us to share in the table of appetizers which had been prepared by some of the town's chefs especially for our welcome. There were trays of canapés or—as the Italians call them— "tartine." I asked my interpreter hostess to ask the chef to describe the canapés and other foods that were on the appetizer table.

"Questo signore vuole sapere come si chiama?" she asked ("This gentleman would like to identify the appetizers").

These were small, thin slices of white bread, measuring about three by four inches, with the crusts removed. There were tartine with generous spreads of either black or red caviar (caviale) decorated with swooshes of mayonnaise; tartine of smoked salmon (salmone) and tartine of steamed baby shrimps (gamberetti).

And much more: salami cremonese, a typical salami of Cremona, and provolone cheese, even frittata (egg omelet) with carote (carrots) e cipolle (and onions).

The tartine fascinated me. I asked for the recipe, and the chef was most gracious:

■ *TARTINE al SALMONE (Salmon Canapes)*
  (serves 4 to 6)

4 ounces smoked salmon
6 tablespoons sweet butter
1/3 cup of freshly grated
  parmesan cheese
1 teaspoon lemon juice
6 pitted olives
2 slices of bread, 1/2 inch
  thick, 3 by 4 inches

• Blend all ingredients except the olives in a food processor or blender. Spread on a slice of bread. Garnish by placing a black olive in the center of each tartine. For shrimp tartine use the same recipe, replacing salmon with shrimp.

As we savored the delicious tartine, the mayor introduced his staff and then for an encore led us into another room which contained display cases of musical instruments, all guarded by an intricate security system. This was the "Salon of the Violins," a room holding the masterpieces of the Cremonese lute-making art. There was the violin known as "Il Cremonese," made by Antonio Stradivari in 1715; another, "L'Hammerle," crafted by Nicolo Amati in 1658; and one made in 1734 by Giuseppe Guarneri.

How my father would have enjoyed this moment! Although not a musician I have an appreciation for music, and particularly for the violin. When I was a small child my father serenaded me to sleep with a lullaby he played on his violin. I must have been five or six at the time but the memory, rich and selfishly preserved, never fades. When I can I tell the story to friends who seem to share in a joyful moment from my past.

As we left the salon, the chef who had prepared the tartine took me aside and handed me a gift: his recipe for "Risotto alla Milanese." I had earlier asked him for one of the region's favorite risotto recipes. After all, Milan, which was the chief city of this region ,was not only famous for fashion and fast cars but risotto as well.

■ *RISOTTO alla MILANESE*
   (serves 3)
   3½ teaspoons butter
   1 small onion, chopped thinly
   2 teaspoons bone marrow
   ¼ cup white wine
   1½ cups rice (ordinary rice may be used. However, one of the following Italian-grown rice varieties is preferred: Carnaroli, Vialone Nano, Razza 77 or Arborio)
   3½ cups beef stock
   ¼ cup grated parmesan cheese
   generous pinch (¼ teaspoon) of saffron powder or 15 saffron threads which have

been crushed to a powder.

(Note: Saffron is worth more than its weight in gold. One gram or $1/28$ of an ounce retails in some markets for $3.95, or $1,769.60 a pound. Saffron is not displayed with other spices but usually kept under lock and key at the checkout stand or in a nearby locked display case. Also, the bone marrow, while not expensive, is not usually displayed in the meat cases. Simply ask the butcher for several fresh marrow bones that have been cut. At home, scoop out the marrow which is visible in the center. Use a teaspoon as the marrow usually has the consistency of hard butter.)

• *Melt butter in a large heavy pan and sauté chopped onion until transparent and golden. Now add the wine and cook over medium heat until it is reduced. Stir in the uncooked rice and sauté gently in the wine/butter/onion mixture until it begins to brown.*

Pour in one cup of boiling beef stock and continue cooking until the liquid has been absorbed, then add another cup of boiling beef stock. Continue to cook the rice, stirring gently, until all the liquid has been used up and absorbed by the rice. Meanwhile, stir the saffron into the remaining cups of hot liquid and allow to steep for a few minutes.

When the rice is ready or almost ready (about 15–20 minutes) add the liquid-soaked saffron, stirring it into the rice, which will color it to a yellowish tinge. Not all the rice may change in color but the flavor of the saffron will be throughout. Turn off the heat. Now thoroughly and gently stir in the remaining butter and the cheese. Cover the pan and let settle for about five minutes or less. Serve immediately.

I soon learned that many of the restaurants we visited featured the rice, which is undoubtedly a favorite of the region.

The next day in Cremona was a mixture of classical art, architecture and food almost impossible to comprehend. One building in Cremona which offers a link to the most creative tradition of this region is the cathedral, or duomo, an example of 12th-century Lombard-Romanesque style. The cathedral has one of the finest towers in Italy, the "Torrazzo," 400 feet in height. It is easy to see that this region and, in fact, most of Italy, has an abundance of priceless art and architectural possessions dating back to the early centuries of the first millennium A.D.

Even the piazza of the cathedral is understood to be a work of art. As the writer Lucia Ramella of Cremona stated in her book on the meaning of the piazza:

"The piazza is to be understood as a dialogue, and so the cross-references from one side to the other pose questions to the tourist, so they suggest meditations for every inhabitant of Cremona.

"But the narrative of the centuries and my emotions does not end here.

"At this strategic crossroads, every citizen of Cremona becomes one of us, a citizen, an irreplaceable and indispensable part of the formation of a community, a city, and a church.

"The Piazza."

Herman Hesse, another writer, in his book *A Day's Journey in Italy* (1913) said the piazza and "the cathedral appeared as a homogenous whole, pervaded by an exquisitely musical intoned musicality," declaring it the most beautiful in the world.

One of my really happy moments in Cremona was the last evening of our two-day visit in that city, walking with my colleagues down one of its many narrow streets, passing shops full of exquisite Italian clothing, and on our way to another restaurant of impeccable cuisine. That evening we dined at the Ristorante Martinelli. There we tasted again some of Cremona's famous salami; then, for the "primi piatti" (first dish) was ricotta and spinach ravioli. It was like something my mother would have prepared for me as a treat for doing my chores and not causing her undue stress (as I often innocently would do in my restless adolescence). Again I asked the proprietor for the recipe, and without hesitation he obliged. As we were leaving he handed me a handwritten note containing the essential ingredients for the ravioli. He called it "Malfatti di ricotta e spinaci" or ravioli with ricotta and

spinach (badly made)—the latter referring only to the form of the ravioli and not the taste! Here is the recipe:

■ *MALFATTI DI RICOTTA E SPINACI*
(serves 4)
Filling:
4 pounds of spinach
1 pound fresh ricotta cheese
grated Parmesan cheese as needed
2 eggs
pinch of grated nutmeg
pinch of salt

* *Boil spinach, drain well and chop fine. Add ricotta, parmesan cheese, eggs, nutmeg, salt as needed and mix all ingredients well.*

Pasta:
2 pounds unbleached flour
6 or 8 whole eggs
pinch of salt

* *Preparation: Knead the pasta and with rolling pin make into a sheet. Cut the pasta in squares, spoon in filling, seal sides. The size and shape of the ravioli is up to the maker, thus the name "Malfatti," indicating odd sizes and shapes.*
Cook ravioli in boiling water until they float to top or until tender. Serve with a cream sauce.

It was now farewell, or "ciao," to Cremona. Here is a city which gave the world the finest of violin makers, architecture of Renaissance beauty, Romanesque statues and Gothic finesse, and a cathedral embroidered with stoneworks of figures, arches and spiral curves—and, above all, probably one of the most important female Renaissance painters, Sofonisba Anguissola, who now seems to be regaining world attention as a result of two exhibitions in Vienna and Washington. Rediscovered after more than 400 years, she will certainly be the rage in the next millennium.

Now the flavor of Italy becomes even more real. Once passed through the lens of our first few days, our impressions are even more magnified. Italy is not a dream...not just pages from history flashing before your eyes. When you leave Italy you may think it was a dream; when you are in Italy the stimulation makes you feel very much alive.

ANTONIO STRADIVARI

Our next stop was Mantova, about 30 miles or so to the east of Cremona. Many Italians, I'm told, rate the cuisine of Mantova among the best with the traditional dishes of Italy. The beginnings of this city are rooted in legend, dating back to the time of the Etruscans, and history claims this was the birthplace of the Latin poet Virgil.

Mantova, or Mantua as the Italians know it, was an important trading center during Roman times. Subsequently it was invaded by the Visigoths and other tribes from the north and northwest. The Visigoths ruled for many centuries and swept southward even to the southern Appennines of the Kingdom of Naples. (I was once told, during a visit to Naples, that some of my ancestors may have been Visigoths. That would account for the blue-eyed paternal grandfather in my family—probably the only northern gene that traveled through the generations. However, there has been no evidence of any Teutonic kitchen skills being passed on through any of those immigrant genes!).

Mantova was a brief stop, but one which I will remember for its cuisine that Sunday afternoon, and also for that rotund member of the cloth who reproved one of my colleagues for wearing his baseball cap while inside the Basilica di Santa Andrea. To my friend such a mild discourtesy was not intentional; in his faith the male is required to wear a head cover. And he was obviously enraptured with the beauty of the artwork inside the basilica, not thinking of the dress code.

The Basilica of Santa Andrea is a most sacred place, for it holds the treasured vases containing some of Christ's blood collected at the bottom of the cross. The chronicles of Charlemagne's court recorded the event in 804; according to the tradition it was collected at the site by a Roman soldier who had pierced the chest of Christ with his lance.

This relic is worshipped on Good Friday, the day that celebrates that very event of the Christian faith. On that day the relic is taken out of the crypt during a complex ceremony and is taken along the streets of the city in a night procession.

Another remarkable feature of this city were the gardens and the succession of scenes which greeted us at the Palazzo Te. In the early 1300s, the long reign of the Gonzaga royal family embellished the city and the surroundings with the height of artistic fervor. Under the patronage of Isabella d'Este (1474–1539), the wife of Francesco II, works were commissioned from Leonardo da Vinci, Giovanni Bellini and the very talented student of Raphael, Giulio Romano, who was given carte blanche to construct and decorate all the buildings. Through his genius Mantova was given a place of major significance in the world of art.

From this came the Palazzo Te, a pleasure house built for entertainment and banquets, with loggias, gardens and grottoes. It was considered one of the wonders of its time. The view of the buildings and gardens, as I personally saw it, was so compelling that my fellow journalists and I simply walked almost reverently throughout this idyllic structure and gazed for what was a very long moment at the power of its beauty.

Gardens of the Palazzo Te

After the tour we were taken to the Ristorante Rigoletto in Mantova. Here the proprietor, Stefano Spezia, treated us to agnoli (similar to Chinese won ton or potstickers) in a fine chicken broth. He also presented us with some of the region's favorite red table wine, Analotta, which is produced on a limited scale. The vintner uses only his own grapes, and releases only 1,000 bottles annually .

We also were served tortelli di zucca (ravioli with pumpkin). This is a prestigious pasta dish of this city. The specialty is made from a pumpkin filling mixed with mustarded compote, macaroons and parmesan cheese served with a melted butter and cheese sauce. Pumpkin is used liberally here in the north in many of its pasta dishes. I found the use of pumpkin as a filling for ravioli quite tasty, particularly when the pasta was served with a cheese sauce. Pumpkin here in the north is known as a food of romance.

■ *TORTELLI DI ZUCCA*

(serves 4)

Filling:
2 pounds of pumpkin (squash)
5 ounces of amaretti, reduced to fine crumbs
1 egg
fine breadcrumbs
5 ounces of mostarda di Mantova (piquant apple relish)
chopped fine nutmeg

Pasta:
2½ cups of flour
¾ cup of semola
2 tablespoons milk
4 eggs

• *Slice the squash, removing the seeds. Bake until soft but not dry. Allow to cool, then remove the rind and purée the squash.*

In a bowl mix the purée with the mostarda and amaretti crumbs, Grana cheese, and a pinch of nutmeg. Add the breadcrumbs as needed to make the mixture firm.

19

Blend well, cover and set aside in cool place for several
hours. Now, make the pasta dough and roll it out.

Cut the dough in rectangles measuring 1½ by 3 inches.
Shape the filling into small balls and place a ball on one
half of the pasta rectangle, pulling the other half over to
cover, pressing the edges together to seal them. Cook in
boiling salted water. The pasta is done when the tortelli rise
to the top. Drain and serve with melted butter and Grana
cheese.

There is another favorite pasta serving which generates,
according to town publicists, competition between mothers-in-
laws and daughters-in-law. This dish, known as "agnolini," is
traditionally served on Christmas Eve. It is a butterfly-shaped
pasta filled with a mixture of pounded meats—beef and pork.
This is a version of the tortellini whose recipe appears in the
chapter on Bologna.

There is much more to see in Mantova, treasures be-
queathed by the Gonzaga family for future generations to enjoy.
But we had to move on, because there was much more to see, and
little time in which to see it.

A sunny afternoon in Parma's plaza

PARMA

It was here in Parma that we finally rested for a few hours in the sunny plaza, staring like little children at the wonderful sights passing by. There are young women in Parma; there are middle-aged women; and there are young children. All have one thing in common: their attire. Tailored. Fashionable. Enviable. The men? Equally tailored. But it was the women—the middle-aged women, particularly—who reminded me of my dear mother, who always made certain her dress for outdoors was impeccable. Arm in arm they walked briskly in the April afternoon sun, chatting, smiling, enjoying each other's company. They circled the plaza, not once but many times. It was like a ritual; a social thing. This was outdoor theater.

Now it was time for me to have some simple food from an ordinary restaurant, nothing pre-planned as had been the previous sumptuous meals arranged by our genial hosts. On the menu, I read what I wanted—a pasta, penne with fresh tomatoes and butter and oil sauce, sprinkled with grated cheese.

■ *PENNE WITH RAW TOMATOES*
(serves 4 to 6)
1/2 pound of fresh, ripe plum tomatoes
1 pound of penne pasta
1/3 cup of olive oil
1 cup freshly grated parmesan cheese
salt to taste

• *Cut the tomatoes lengthwise, remove the seeds and dice.*

Cook the pasta about 6 minutes or until "al dente"—don't overcook.

Drain and transfer the pasta to a serving bowl. Pour the olive oil, the grated cheese and the diced tomatoes over the pasta, toss thoroughly and serve.

As I savored this delightful interlude I enjoyed the continuing parade of smartly dressed Parmaseans.

Following lunch we met with the mayor of Parma, Dr. Stefano Lavagetto, an interesting combination of a relaxed academic and a courtly member of a 15th-century Venetian court. He was impressive, a quiet man who was an avid listener. I was told he was an extremely liberal person, not uncommon in this northern country of avowed anti-fascists.

"We have to offer in Parma more than just cheese and prosciutto," said the mayor with a slightly visible smile on his face. "Parma is a classical town," he went on. "Many years ago it was the center for travelers."

An apartment building in Parma

Yes, there is more to Parma than ham and cheese. After all, Parma was the home of great musical genius. Arturo Toscanini, one of the world's great musical conductors, was born here. The musical soul of Parma also identifies itself with Giuseppe Verdi and Niccolo Paganini. While America was reportedly taming the West, Italy was giving the world another Renaissance in the form of music.

Parma is also rich in the precious works of art nurtured by the Farnese and Bourbon dynasties. It is a city of some 170,000 people whose history goes back to the time of the Romans. There are castles and other buildings of historic value which gave me a deeper insight into this community.

One of the treats of visiting Parma, and unfortunately one that I was not able to take advantage of, was the spas; on the next trip this is something I will definitely take in. I'm told that for sheer magnificence, the Terme Berzieri spa building in Salsomaggiore is a worthy rival to the baths of ancient Rome. Salsomaggiore, just northwest of Parma, is a spa of international renown. The salty, iodinic waters of springs there were first used in the second century B.C. as a source of common salt.

———————

Nevertheless, one of the greatest attractions in Parma, and there are many, is its culinary tradition. Here in this region of Italy it is often said that cooking "is an art to which creators and consumers are equally devoted." Nowhere is this more striking than in Parma which, after Bologna, is the most interesting and unusual town in the Emilia-Romagna region.

I do wonder sometimes why food fails to ignite passion in people. I am referring not to gluttony but to true appreciation of food which is prepared with loving care. I always tell my students that preparing food for someone is a real expression of affection.

Even those who remain unexcited about food are aware of some of the products which come from this city. Who hasn't heard of Parmesan cheese? Or prosciutto? Not just ordinary prosciutto, but the prosciutto of Parma, cured by farmers whose skill comes from centuries of tradition in the art of curing ham.

One thing to remember is that not all parmesan cheese is the authentic product, which is sold only under the label of Parmigiano-Reggiano. In the introduction to a booklet I received at the dairy consortium in Parma, Marcella Hazan, who teaches in nearby Bologna, wrote that "good ingredients handled simply is what Italian food is all about, and no single product more perfectly epitomizes the character of good Italian cooking than Parmigiano-Reggiano."

For most people, according to Marcella Hazan, " 'parmesan' just means hard cheese used for grating." However, she explained, there is a world of difference between generic 'parmesan' and the real product Parmigiano-Reggiano, the difference that has always existed between an imitation and the real thing. Simply look for the brand on the package and you will be certain of getting the real thing.

You might ask yourself: How do you use all this grated cheese? This answer is: preferably on pastas such as lasagne, tortellini, tagliatelle, ziti, penne and, as my dear mother often did, also on different soups such as chicken, beef and, of course, minestrone, to name but a few. I see too many diners overdosing on grated cheese on practically every type of pasta dish, even going so far as to sprinkle cooked greens with grated cheese. Basta—enough!—already. Grated cheese augments the flavor of the dish. It is not intended to submerge the true taste of the main food item.

Here is a recipe for grated cheese in a mixed salad supplied by the Parmigiano-Reggiano cooperative and provided by Giorgio Fini:

■ *MIXED SALAD*
(serves 4 to 6)
one head of romaine lettuce (average size)
5 or 6 red radishes, sliced
2 diced celery hearts
1 finocchio sliced thin
4 ounces Parmigiano-Reggiano cheese, cut in slivers
2 tablespooons olive oil
1 tablespoon balsamic vinegar
salt to taste

• *Combine all ingredients thoroughly and serve.*

Here is another favorite recipe given to me by the Parmesan cheese cooperative which combines the two culinary food stars of the region—ham (prosciutto) and cheese:

■ *RIGATONI WITH PROSCIUTTO or boiled ham*
(serves 4 to 6)
6 ounces of boiled ham, diced
4 ounces whole milk mozzarella, diced
1 cup of cream
1 pound of rigatoni
6 ounces of freshly grated Parmigiano-Reggiano cheese
salt
2 tablespoons of butter

• *Put the ham and mozzarella in a saucepan. Add the cream and grated cheese. Turn on the heat and over low flame or low heat cook for just a few minutes until the cream is reduced slightly. Cook the rigatoni in boiling water until "al dente" or firm to bite and then drain.*

Pour pasta into a butter-smeared baking dish and add the white sauce and toss thoroughly.

Place in an oven preheated to 400° and bake for 15 minutes. Serve within a few minutes.

One evening we dined without the company of dignitaries, remaining in our hotel for dinner. We were staying at the Grand Hotel Baglioni, which is located within walking distance of Parma's town center and is a favorite of the local business community. The food prepared for us in one of its elegant dining rooms immortalized for me the memory of that evening with my compatriots. The hotel restaurant was the Canova; the chef was Frederico Del Sante.

Chef Frederico Del Sante

The meal opened with the usual, "il prosciutto di Parma," something which was not absent from any of our meals during the week-long visit. There is absolutely nothing to compare with the prosciutto of Parma. Though costly, it leaves you with a taste that lingers with pleasure. Then we were served a risotto alla parmigiana or rice with grated cheese. The supreme treat was salmon. It was steamed salmon with sweet and sour courgettes (like zucchini).

Here I feel that I can make a fair judgment of salmon because of living for so many years in the Pacific Northwest, the home of the great Columbia River Chinook salmon. Chef Del Sante said that he used Norwegian salmon and seasoned it with olive oil, garlic cloves, some white wine and a sprinkling of thyme and marjoram. It was steamed until tender. Sometimes I prefer steamed or poached fish to baked or grilled. The gentler cooking tends to preserve the flavors and makes the fish more succulent, eliminating the need of adding strong condiments which I feel generally compete with the true taste of the meat.

Parma will always remain a special city for me, not only for its food, but for the evidence I saw of a city rich in an aristocratic cultural tradition. Some of the celebrated artists who worked there ranged from Benedetto Antelami to Salimbene, from Correggio to Parmigiannino, from Bodoni to Verdi and Toscanini. The grand works of architecture deeply impressed me such as the ca-

The cultural traditions of the theatre have been observed in Parma for centuries.

thedral and Baptistery, truly gems of their periods and treasures to behold even to this day.

Other famous names were part of this historic city. In the Middle Ages it was already a flourishing town ruled by the Visconti, the Sforza, the French and the Papacy from the 14th to 16th centuries. In 1545 a Duchy was established by Pope Paul III, who installed his son Pier Luigi Farnese as its ruler. It was a dynasty that ruled for almost two centuries. In the first half of the 18th century the Duchy was inherited by the Bourbons, who brought a French flavor to the court. Even to this day, the remnants of French ways still seem to be jealously adhered to, thereby establishing in their minds a sort of cultural zone of demarcation from the South.

Palazzo Ducale, Modena

MODENA

The name does not seem difficult to pronounce. In Italy, though, I found that I was mispronouncing it, placing the accent on the latter part of the name. It is not "moDENA" but "MOdena."

This was the first lesson I learned when I arrived in Modena. Another was that there is more to this city located in the middle of Emilia Romagna region than its widely-known elixir of culinary enthusiasts—"aceto balsamico" or balsamic vinegar.

The first traces of civilization in this area are of the Etruscans, which date back to between the 6th and 4th centuries B.C. The name of the city comes from the Celtic word "Mouden," referring to the city's position at the foot of the surrounding hills.

There is a masculinity about Modena and its environs which is evident in a number of places, including the country's main military academy, the Accademia Militare—the West Point of Italy. The academy is located in the Palazzo Ducale, a former castle which offers an example of 17th century secular architecture.

Also in the vicinity of Modena is the community of Maranello, the home of the Galleria Ferrari, a tribute to Italy's proud contribution to the world of fine automobiles. What a vi-

Ferrari Formula One

sual feast! There I saw the 125—the first car built by Enzo Ferrari—and the F50, the only Formula One car, which was produced in just 349 units. These are just some significant examples of Ferrari genius on exhibit. There is a sensuality about such machines that go beyond the ability for verbal description. I mentioned my visit to Ferrari to an acquaintance, a racing car enthusiast, and the expression on his face as I related to him the excitement of my visit was comparable to that of an art lover's first encounter with the Mona Lisa.

But there is more. The motor industry here today still includes the famous names of De Tomaso, Bugatti and Maserati. Some car lovers in America may not be aware that the legendary Bugatti returned to production in 1990 after an absence of 51 years. The Bugatti company produces the EB 110 Supersport. The De Tomaso firm, set up in 1959 by former Argentinian racing driver Alejandro De Tomaso, produces the Pantera coupe, which is available in Europe, Japan, and the Arab countries. And if you really want a treat: Every Saturday afternoon, by appointment only, groups may be invited to visit the Ferrari Club Maranello.

The more you see of the Modena area the more extraordinary it becomes. Everything overwhelms. Even nearby Carpi becomes too much to comprehend. Here in Carpi the textile and clothing industries account for a total of 5,000 businesses, most of which are very small with an average of five employes per business. The clothiers operate exclusively in the field of knitwear. This is part of what makes Italy an economic power.

If the excitement of Modena becomes too much for you, only minutes away is the Salvarola Terme, a thermal waters resort about ten miles from Modena, near the small community of Sassuolo. Relaxing in thermal waters was one of the most enjoyable memories of an earlier visit to Italy, a trip I had taken several years before to the island of Ischia, the sister island to Capri but not as familiar to most Americans.

In Ischia I bathed in the Island's coastal Mediterranean waters, bobbing like a child in a warm bath as waiters waded out to me to serve mussels fetched from the rocks and boiled in a nearby natural thermal pool. With each succulent morsel I was given sips of Ischia's fine white wine, crushed from grapes grown on the island volcanic slopes. How idyllic the moment...how everlasting the memory has been.

The author with Ermes Malpighi and a cask of aged vinegar

Although not as idyllic, the visit to a Modena farm where another type of grape is grown, the trebbiano, brought me a great deal of satisfaction. It was the farm cooperative that produces the balsamic vinegar. My meeting was with one of the growers, Ermes Malpighi, who greeted me and my companions at the entrance to one of the storage buildings where the traditional balsamic vinegar of Modena is stored.

There is a charm about the farm that provided me with a different impression than I usually get when visiting areas of agricultural production. I spent many years writing about farming in the Pacific Northwest and have some insight into this type of life. However, here it was more of a "gentleman farm" atmosphere. The employees or supervisory staff would easily be at home in a big-city high rise office. The owner was impeccably dressed and his assistants, probably family members, were equally suave in appearance.

The grounds more resembled an estate than a farm. We entered one small building and were ushered upstairs where we saw, for the first time, rows upon rows of neatly stacked darkened barrels containing the aromatic balsamic vinegar. The pleasant aroma of the fermenting vinegar was almost hypnotic.

I felt that such a working environment would be easy to take regardless of how long the hours were.

Mr. Malpighi told us that the trebbino grape must, or pulp for fermentation, is obtained by a boiling procedure, which results in a high sugar content. Then, in order to ensure the correct process of acetification and aging, the must remains in wood casks for a long period of time. The aging process, which may take years, results in a highly pungent perfumed product which sells for steep prices. I purchased a small attractive bottle containing no more than five ounces for about $50. My vinegar had been aged for 15 years. A fellow journalist bought a 25-year-old vinegar for $75. Now, there are in stores quart bottles of the vinegar which sell for only several dollars, but these are not aged or handled using the same delicate process. However, the latter do have the balsamic flavor.

The aged vinegar is used more like syrup on ice cream. In fact, we did have several drops on gelati which had been prepared by the owner. In addition, he provided us with trays of strawberries to which he carefully added several drops of the

Our first day: the reception at Il Palazzo Communale in Cremona

Tartine al Salmone, page 11

above: Malfatti di Ricotta, page 15
left: Risotto alla Milanese, page 12

Cremona is famed for its numerous churches and cathedrals, beautifully decorated with murals, carvings and woodwork.

Another view of Mantova's Palazzo Te

Stefano Spezia's agnoli in chicken broth, page 19

Penne with Raw Tomatoes, page 21

Giorgio Fini's mixed salad, page 24

Not just ordinary prosciutto, but the prosciutto of Parma!

Lasagne with Béchamel Sauce, page 51

The Baptistery, Parma

Piazza Grande in Modena

Looking through the gate into the courtyard of Palazzo Ducale, Modena

The Palazzo Ducale is now the site of the Accademia Militare, the Italian equivalent of West Point.

The Galeria Ferrari in Maranello, near Modena

The markets of Bologna are many and richly varied.

Tortellini of Bologna, served in broth, page 54

Silverio Cineri's roast beef with arugula, page 56

*Above and below: Silverio's
antique tools and chafing dish*

*Silverio's
Ristorante,
Bologna*

*A synagogue
in Ferrara*

A typical archway

A

GIROLAMO SAVONAROLA

IN TEMPI CORROTTI E SERVILI

DEI VIZI E DEI TIRANNI

FLAGELLATORE

Savonarola, the "Mad Monk" who was burned for heresy, is commemorated by a statue in his home town of Ferrara.

Mosaicists' gallery in Ravenna

A restoration artist works pains-takingly to repair an ancient mosaic.

One of Ravenna's many splendid mosaics, undergoing restoration.

aged balsamic, giving it an exotic semi-sweet flavor. The same application can be used on certain specially prepared greens. What a treat!

But there is more. Here are some ways—suggested by the Balsamic Vinegar Cooperative of Modena—in which the aged vinegar can be used as a sublime accompaniment to many dishes:

■ *FOR APERITIF TIME:*
• *Pour several drops of Balsamic vinegar over thin chips of parmesan cheese. After wrapping thin slices of prosciutto around breadsticks, arrange them on a serving plate and sprinkle with several drops of balsamic vinegar.*

■ *FOR HORS D'OEUVRE:*
• *Prepare a bed of salad, chopped as needed, on a serving platter. Brown some bacon in a sauté pan and put it in the center of the serving platter. Dress with olive oil and balsamic vinegar as desired.*

■ *FOR THE FIRST COURSE:*
• *Prepare a mixture of bacon and onion. Transfer to a sauté pan with olive oil, butter and a bouquet garni of aromatic herbs. Set it aside to flavor the mixture.*

Sprinkle with one teaspoon of balsamic vinegar and add two tablespoons of stock. Season with salt and pepper and cook it over moderate heat until dense. Cook "tagliatelle' (a pasta in ribbon form) to the point at which it is al dente. Drain the pasta and transfer it to a soup tureen. Add the sauce and sprinkle with Parmesan cheese.

■ *FOR THE SECOND COURSE:*
• *Finely chop an onion and sauté it in a pan with olive oil. Beat two to three eggs in a mixing bowl with Parmesan cheese, salt and pepper. Pour the beaten eggs over the browned onion and finish cooking the eggs. Serve with a generous amount of Balsamic vinegar.*

■ *WITH DESSERT:*
• *Wash some strawberries and place them in a bowl. Sprinkle with sugar and allow them to rest until a sweet*

sauce forms. When ready to serve, complete with a sprinkle of balsamic vinegar and garnish with fresh mint leaves.

To make vanilla ice cream more original, serve with several drops of Balsamic vinegar.

This last may seem like experimention. But, believe me, the strawberries and ice cream with droplets of balsamic vinegar—the aged version—offer an exciting new taste (not to mention the conversation it creates at a dinner party!). So try it! Live a little!

The wine cellar of the Salumeria deli

Incidentally, Luciano Pavarotti, a native of Modena, has a favorite of veal piccatina with ham sprinkled with balsamic vinegar.

While in Modena I tasted sautéed zucchini that had been sprinkled very lightly with balsamic vinegar. The zucchini had been sautéed in olive oil and butter, then served along with roasted beef. The zucchini had a deep flavor, unlike any zucchini I had tasted before.

At noon on the 8th of April we entered a deli (the Salumeria) stocked with savory foods and immediately were served white and red wines in Austrian crystal glass. Suddenly the tiny elegant shop was filled with visiting dignitaries who had been looking forward, I'm told, to our visit. I was more impressed with the dozens of dangling prosciutto hams and stacks of dried fish and more ham stacked decoratively behind the cases…It was a feast for the eyes. The cases were filled with cheeses of all kinds and meats of all kinds. Bacchus must have anointed this shop. But this was only the beginning, because we were then led to the inner sanctum where an ancient wine cellar was opened for our investigation. Every sort of antique tool for wine making was in there. Adjoining the cellar was what looked liked someone's large dining room. It, too, was furnished with antique furniture, enough to make any merchant of collectibles lust. In here we had our lunch, and it was here that the patrone, Giuseppe Giusti, delicately served, in droplets, very old Balsamic on our sautéed zucchini. Never have I tasted anything like it before.

It was la Signora in the cucina who prepared the feast of lasagne with béchamel sauce. I had the distinct pleasure of gaining entrance into her kitchen, where I apparently was successful in overwhelming her with compliments, hoping she would reward me with her recipe. As the meal was reaching its conclusion, la Signora Mirandi, the chef, emerged and presented me with her recipe, which she had carefully handwritten as we were completing our dessert. It was written in red ink on some scratch paper, but to me it was a priceless memento. This is the recipe:

■ *LASAGNE WITH BÉCHAMEL SAUCE*
(serves 15)
Sauce:
3/4 pound ground pork
3/4 pound ground veal
1/2 cup of olive oil
2 ounces of unsalted butter
1 stalk celery, finely chopped

1 medium carrot, finely chopped
1 medium carrot, finely chopped
2 pounds fresh tomatoes (or large can of tomatoes, drained)

• Combine ingredients and cook at medium heat for 3 hours.

Green pasta:

1¹/2 pounds of unbleached all-purpose flour
6 whole eggs
4 ounces of spinach, boiled and drained

• Mix above ingredients and roll the dough very thin with the rolling pin. Make strips 3 inches wide

Béchamel sauce:

1 quart of whole milk
4 tablespoons of flour
6 ounces of unsalted butter
1 teaspoon of salt and 1 teaspoon nutmeg

• Melt butter, add salt and nutmeg, stir slowly until gold in color, add milk, continue to stir making sure to dissolve lumps, cook at low heat for 12–15 minutes.

Boil lasagne pasta in salted water for three minutes, drain, rinse in cold water, dry.

• In a baking dish combine the following layers:
– a layer of béchamel sauce
– a layer of meat sauce and grated parmesan cheese
– a layer of lasagne
– a layer of béchamel sauce
– a layer of meat sauce and parmesan cheese
• Repeat until the pan is filled. Top with meat sauce and parmesan cheese. Bake at 400° for 45 minutes.

Buon apetito!

BOLOGNA

Many writers have written about Bologna. Many cooks have praised its culinary riches. Waverley Root wrote in *The Cooking of Italy*:

"If Tuscany and Florence offer the purest of cooking, Bologna la grassa—'Bologna the fat'—offers by all odds the richest, and must be considered the gastronomic center of the north." As the 19th-century writer and cooking expert Pellegrino Artusi once said, "When you hear mention made of Bolognese cooking, drop a little curtsy, for it deserves it." The food in Bologna is not only succulent, not only good tasting, but wholesome as well.

The guide on our trip here told us we would be concentrating more on the art and culture of this city than the food. Time was limited; in fact, we were there only a few hours; but in that time we gathered so much material and met so many interesting people that the visit was indeed a spectacular one.

We were in this northern region of Italy for only seven days. I could have stayed seven days in Bologna and it still would not satisfy me. It does not matter how long you stay here, it is never long enough; Bologna is too immense. Although it is a city of a half million people, about the size of my own city of Portland, Oregon, there is limitless sense of activity here. Trying to harvest every aspect of life in Bologna can be a powerful, yet exhausting journey.

Walking through Bologna's restaurant district, I was captivated by the displays of foods in the windows. This well-fed city has a reputation for its rich style of cooking. But it seems to boast most about its tortellini and tagliatelle—the latter a pasta first served on the table of a nobleman who was inspired by the flaxen hair of his principal guest, Lucrezia Borgia. Tortellini, though it does not have such a romantic history, is nevertheless a favorite of many Bolognese households. These are small rings of dough stuffed with such things as pork, turkey, prosciutto and egg yolks. They are boiled and then served in consomme or with ragu and grated cheese or with butter and cream and grated cheese. A Christmas dinner in Bologna traditionally begins with tortellini.

■ *TAGLIATELLE (ribbon noodles)*
(serves 2)
1 cup plain white flour
1 egg
few drops of water
pinch of salt

• *Sift the flour onto a pastry board and make a well in the center. Break the egg, drop into the well and mix the egg, flour, water and salt with fingertips or a fork. Work the dough. It will be difficult at first, but after about 15 minutes or so of kneading it will become pliable. (I prefer a little music in the background which will alleviate the boredom of kneading. A glass of wine will also soothe the kneading process.) Roll the dough into a ball and let it rest for about 20 minutes, covering it with a cloth or a bowl.*

Roll the dough out into paper-thin sheets, using a rolling pin. Then roll up the dough until it is about two inches wide. Use a sharp knife and cut into rounds of about ½ inch wide, then open and spread on to a board to dry. Cook in boiling water or chicken stock until tender (about three minutes) and serve with melted butter and parmesan cheese.

■ *TORTELLINI OF BOLOGNA*
Prepare the dough the same as for tagliatelle. However, as

soon as the dough is rolled out, cut it into two-inch circles. After wetting the edges of a circle, lay the filling on the top. Fold over; the wet edges will stick together. Gently press the edges together with your fingertips, making certain the filling will not leak out. Now wrap the filled dough around your left index finger so that the two ends curl around and overlap slightly. They should be pressed firmly together and turned upwards. This will be the ring of the tortellini, what in Italian is known as a "little hat."

To cook. drop tortellini in boiling water which has been lightly salted and cooked until done, about three to four minutes. Serve with meat sauce, or in hot beef or chicken broth.

The usual stuffing is a paste of prosciutto, mortadella, veal and parmesan cheese, with a dash of nutmeg. A chicken filling can also be used. The following is the recipe for the chicken filling.

■ CHICKEN TORTELLINI FILLING
(serves 4)
1 cup chopped cooked chicken, preferably breast poached in chicken stock for about 15 minutes.
1/4 cup of freshly grated parmesan cheese
1 egg yolk, beaten
1/16 teaspoon grated lemon peel
pinch of nutmeg
pinch of salt
pinch of black pepper

Bologna shops feature tortellini of all varieties.

• Mix the ingredients in a large bowl until they are thoroughly combined. Then begin filling the dough, about ¹/₄ teaspoon of mixture in the center of each round of dough.

The tortellini are best if cooked at once, but they can be covered with a damp cloth or plastic wrap and refrigerated for a day or two.

———

One of the finest chefs of Bologna, Silverio Cineri, operates the Silverio Ristorante, a restaurant with a reputation that goes beyond the borders

The author with Silverio Cineri

of this region and in fact has received acclaim from writers throughout Europe and other parts of the world.

I was unaware of the popularity of this restaurant, nor had we been told that the owner and chef was a talented and highly respected member of the culinary guild of this community.

The lunch at Silverio began with tortellini in brodo (broth) followed by pure magic: lasagne al forno (baked lasagne) and slices of roast beef, done medium, garnished with arugula and seasoned lightly with balsamic vinegar.

Roast beef garnished with arugula

When I met Silverio he reminded me of a more youthful and thinner Luciano Pavarotti. As we first entered the restaurant Silverio did not make himself too obvious. We had been accompanied there by our guides and several of the city dignitaries. It was his way, I think, of relinquishing the "stage" to the visiting community leaders rather than hog the visit. However, as we got into the lunch we learned more about our host chef and also of this city, which has survived many tragic wars, including World War II.

Talking to Silverio in the privacy of his kitchen as my colleagues were enjoying their creme al caffe, I learned much about his culinary history. He showed me books, cookbooks, dating back to 800 A.D.. One of the most intriguing exhibits was his collection of old, very old, and rare cooking utensils. One item from his collection was a small, roughly handcarved wooden handle, the length of a pencil and about twice as thick. He showed that to me and then pointed to the protruding metal symbol at one end. He said this was a bread stamp used on uncooked loaves of bread for identification purposes. It was the Nazi swastika. (The German armed forces were in this area during World War II as war partners with the Italian Fascist regime.)

We talked some more, even though there was difficulty in understanding; my Italian is brutally bad, and his Italian is so exemplary. Fortunately, his wife knew some English and therefore we were able to communciate somewhat. At the time I did not have my tape recorder activated, as my hands were busy taking photographs of him in the kitchen.

He was uneasy at first, but then as we got more involved in our photo shoot he began to relax. He gradually grasped my sincere interest in his line of work and that seemed to please him. I then asked him for a recipe, any recipe, which I could use in my forthcoming book about this trip. He left the kitchen for a minute and returned with a beautiful book which he had written called *Cucina Poetica ("Poetry in the Kitchen")*.

I asked for a copying machine so that I could make a copy of one of the recipes. He shook his head, indicating "no," and then handed me the book. His wife explained that the book was a gift to me. I could not believe it. It was a beautifully crafted book of poetry and recipes and he autographed it "A Giuseppe, ringraziando" ("To Joseph, with much thanks"). At that moment I was overwhelmed by his gesture almost to the point of tears. I treasured the gift and did not reveal it to my companions knowing that it would be a source of envy.

For those lovers of salmon, here is Silverio's recipe on a delicious salmon spread appetizer:

■ ROBIOLA WITH SALMON
(serves 6)
two 8-ounce packages of cream cheese or similar semisoft cheese
6 ounces of chopped smoked salmon
optional: one tablespoon of chopped onion

• Mix ingredients well to obtain a uniform pink blend. Serve on crostini (tiny slices of toasted bread, either Italian or French).

During this brief visit I did learn that diners in Bologna do not have "spaghetti alla bolognese," a popular item in American restaurants featuring northern Italian cooking. Spaghetti, according to the Bolognese, is the main pasta for those in southern Italy. What is proper for Bologna is "tagliatelle alla Bolognese," using ragu, a combination of vegetables and meat typically called "soffrito." The vegetables and meat are fried first, then fresh tomatoes or tomato paste may be added as an optional ingredient.

Here is a recipe for the ragu, or bolognese meat sauce:

■ RAGU alla BOLOGNESE
(serves 6)
1 finely chopped medium onion
1 finely chopped medium carrot
1 stalk celery, finely chopped
six tablespoons of butter
2 1/2 tablespoons of olive oil
2/3 cup finely chopped bacon
3/4 cup of ground pork

3/4 cup of ground beef
1/4 cup sausage (pork) meat
2/3 cup of dry white wine
salt and pepper to taste
4 teaspoons tomato paste
1 1/4 cups beef stock
4 tablespoons light cream or milk

• *Heat half the butter and all the oil in a deep skillet. Add the bacon, onion, carrot and celery and fry over low heat until the vegetables are soft and begin to change color. Add the beef, pork and sausage meat and fry these together gently until they brown. Moisten with wine and cook until the wine evaporates, then season with salt and pepper.*

Dilute the tomato paste with a little stock. Stir this into the sauce, cover and cook slowly, stirring from time to time, gradually adding the rest of the stock.

After the sauce has cooked for about 1 1/2 hours, stir in the cream or milk and continue cooking until reduced. Add the remaining butter and stir until melted and thoroughly mixed into the sauce.

If you like mushrooms, add chopped mushrooms, about 1/4 pound, flavored with parsley and garlic and sautéed in butter. This may be added at the final moments.

The above would be sufficient for about slightly more than a pound of pasta.

———

While food was not the primary purpose for our visit to Bologna, it certainly made a lasting impression. However, our guide wanted us to see the art and culture which is everywhere in this wonderful city.

This fountain in Bologna displays an earthy sense of humor.

Bologna is considered a legendary capital of higher learning. Why? Because it was here in Bologna that the first university in the western world was founded, in the latter part of the

A Bologna street scene, glimpsed from an arcaded alley

11th century. The city has been called "la dotta," ("the learned one") and even "la turrita" ("the turreted one").

Bologna's mall—a modern piazza

There is definitely much to savor about this historic city. It is a pleasure just to stroll along its medieval avenues and observe the lights and shadows beneath its endless porticoes. You somehow can feel the richness of this city. Had there been a Trevi fountain I would have tossed in a coin wishing for a speedy return.

Cyclist in Ferrara

FERRARA

From my upstairs window at the hotel I found a moment of simple enjoyment watching people working, shopping and bicycling. It was nothing grand. When you have been exposed for the past few days to not one but a series, an unending series of magnificent relics of history, simple things can cause you to stare in wonderment.

It was a narrow street, typical of many in this city. Across from my small but elegant hotel was a tiny food store, the size of a child's bedroom. There was a flurry of activity this particular morning—the early delivery of foodstuffs, crates of fresh vegetables and fruits, and then a steady stream of shoppers, both pedestrians and bicylists. It was people watching. It was picturesque. My eyes were training themselves to seize this moment.

I will always remember the middle-aged woman with the shoulder strap purse, wearing a full-length (mid-calf) cloth coat, who pedaled up to the store, disembarked, entered the shop and reappeared later with a shopping bag of groceries. But, before embarking, she reached into her purse and extracted a Marlboro (everyone in Italy seems to smoke them) and pedaled off, puffing away as traffic weaved in and out around her. Somehow, to me this was a symbol of an urbane cut of life as lived in a city proud of its majestic churches and aristocractic palazzos.

Ferrara was founded in the high Middle Ages. It prospered and expanded into a marketplace and port on the Po River. The House of Este ruled Ferrara from the 13th until the 16th century. Under its rule, architecture and art flourished. One of the most interesting, and by some considered the most beautiful, street in Italy, the Corso Ercole d'Este, was constructed as a private road serving the homes of the duke's family and friends. At the time of construction it was one of the widest, in fact the widest street in all of Italy. and some said it was "as wide as a swollen river flowing toward infinity." On this street is a building, a masterpiece of the Italian Renaissance. I have never seen a building with such construction. The facade is covered with more than 12,000 diamond-shaped stones or ashlars. The effect is remarkable. It looks as if the building is clad in a glittering suit of armour. There is a legend here that inside each ashlar is a real diamond. However, since its construction no one has dared to test the legend.

Wall of diamond-shaped stones

Inside this "diamond-clustered" building, originally built in the 15th century by Biagio Rossetti as the Palazzo dei Diamanti ("Diamond Palace"), is the National Gallery of Ferrara. It was here that we took an unexpected detour from our appointed tour rounds. On display were the artistic works of the famous Italian director Michelangelo Antonioni. It was the first complete show of all Antonioni's production of paintings from the 1960s to the 1980s. A printed statement by Antonioni which was available at the exhibit read, in part:

"The most curious aspect of my pictorial experience is that, while I am painting, I don't feel like a painter." He said his painting gave him a freedom and feeling of relief because he was not near problems and ideas regarding his work.

There is something about living in the plains of the Po River Valley that has encouraged artists of all kinds to greatness.

Further along the Corso Ercole I d'Este is one of the

principal sights of this city, the Estense Castle, built in 1385. It is a symbol not only of the city but also of the ruling d'Este family who lived in an era of splendour and intrigue, the latter not unusual in Italian lore.

I crossed the moat via a drawbridge, entered this castle and walked the narrow cobblestone corridors down deep below the water's surface to the dungeons where Giulio d'Este was imprisoned for 56 years. Despite the years of confinement he had not lost his sensitivity. Upon his release his first thoughts, according to legend, were of the fair splendour of the hair of Lucrezia Borgia, once Duchess of Ferrara. She was no more, having died 40 years before his release.

The dungeon of the Estense Castle

Scale model of the fortifications that once protected Ferrara

In this castle another drama of passion has survived through the centuries and was related to us by our hosts as we trudged through the remaining narrow corridors of the castle. Apparently the young wife of Nicolo III, Parisina, and the prince's equally young son, Ugo, were caught "in the act of adultery" and were imprisoned and beheaded. George Byron wrote about this sad and romantic story in the poem "Parisina."

———————

By our sixth day we had begun to be somewhat jaded by the staggering number of duomos—churches and cathedrals—in this region of Emilia-Romagna. Each was precious and they were all great buildings, a perpetual tribute to the builders and architects of the period. However, when you see so many, one after the other, you begin to lose your ability to differentiate among them. We visited something in Ferrara, though, that revitalized our group and gave us a new perspective on religious life in this city.

The discovery of this different cultural entity was important because it gave us a deeper insight into the people of Ferrara. There had been a cosmopolitan aura about this city, particularly noticeable when we first checked into our hotel, the Duchessa Isabella. The Duchessa reminded me of an "establishment" type of hotel, catering to those who prefer a continental atmosphere and service.

In the city of Ferrara is a thriving Jewish community which was, and after five centuries still is, an important contributor to the area's social, cultural and business life.

Ferrara, we were told, has several synagogues and a Jewish cemetery. We were taken to the section of the city where the ghetto was located and also to the site of one of the synagogues. Seeing the synagogue and walking through the streets of the ghetto gave me, and I am sure also my colleagues, a feeling of sadness, knowing what must have taken place here in this beautiful city during the terrible days of World War II. Much of this region was in control of enemy forces.

After the tour we were taken to La Romantica trattoria on the Via Ripagrande, where we enjoyed an Italian holiday-type meal highlighted with the region's famous cappelletti (similar to the tortellini on page 55) in chicken broth, followed by roasted wild fowl with small potatoes browned and salted lightly. The wine served was a favorite of Ferrara known as Bosco Iliceo, made from grapes similar to Bordeaux. During the lunch I got better acquainted with one of our hosts for the trip, a gentleman from Ferrara, Nicola Gigli. I asked him whether he was related to the other famous Gigli whose first name was Beniamino (in English, Benjamin). Nicola said Beniamino Gligi was his uncle. He told me when he was a small child the

elder Gigli came to his house and used to pick him up and sing to him. Nicola was unaware at the time of Beniamino's worldwide reputation as an opera singer. This was another testimony to the culture of this region.

Our final evening was celebrated with a performance in a private dining room of the hotel where a beautiful cast of dancers dressed in a Renaissance theme displayed their versatility for our enjoyment. And with that we bid "adieu" to Ferrara.

Ferrara street scene

Dante's Tomb

RAVENNA

When I arrived in Ravenna with my colleagues and hosts I was not adequately prepared for this fresh and generous city. I knew little of the history, the art and the city's other treasures that were shown to us.

All the world knows of Dante; hardly anyone in the outside world knows of Ravenna. It is an undiscovered fairyland which at one time many centuries ago, around the 5th century A.D., was the last capital of the Roman Empire in the west. And it was the the principal center of the Byzantine civilization in Italy during the 6th and 7th centuries.

Dante made Ravenna his home. Here he magnified his praises of the city which had offered him refuge after he fled in 1319 from political antagonists in his beloved Florence.

Dante was buried here in 1321, and his burial place is a perpetual shrine, for here was a poet who knew how to rattle the cage of the establishment. The day that I visited his tomb, a time I will always remember—on April 10, 1997—shortly after 4 p.m., as the sun was setting behind the ornate palazzo walls, the sightseers, the mourners, the literati, flowed continuously in and out of the tomb. The space inside the tomb was rather small and the visiting area could only accommodate about six or seven people at a time. Consequently, there seemed to be continually a flow of visitors in the short period that I was there. That evening we saw a theater poster on one of the buildings announcing a performance of Dante's "Divine Comedy." Dante was still very much alive.

My reason for coming to Ravenna was fulfilled. Now I was ready to leave for home; whatever else there was to see would not equal this experience—or, at least, that is what I thought. But soon I learned differently, for what began to unfold in the remaining hours of our visit were many more undiscovered treasures.

Ravenna has been called an Eastern jewel in a Western setting. For many centuries before other Italian towns and cities, Ravenna "shone with a light in an age that was called dark elsewhere."

Honorius came here in 402 A.D. and made it the heir to Rome, the last capital of the Western Roman Empire. His half-sister Galla Placidia, empress and a Christian, ruled. It was here that the Gothic King Theodoric, raised at the Eastern court and conqueror of Odoacer's Heruli, built his palace and erected the classical churches and buildings that still stand as memorials to his name. And it was here, after the town was retaken by Justinian in 540 A.D., that the Exarchs who ruled for two centuries turned Ravenna into a western Byzantium.

The monuments and memorials all reflect this city's rich and long history.

Part of that treasured past are the mosaics executed in smaltite and marble. I know little of the technique or art of mosaics, only that my experience here in Ravenna would make those less fortunate but more learned envious of my visit. I had been unaware that Ravenna is the mother lode of Christianity's finest mosaics. I was told by one of our host guides (Filippo Bandolini) that nowhere, not even at Constantinople, can one see such a dazzling array of Byzantine mosaics as those which adorn the churches and baptisteries of Ravenna. I was truly overwhelmed by what I saw in those few but memorable hours.

Fortunately, the art of mosaics is not dead. It has had a rebirth in the 20th century. I saw artists skilled in the fine art of restoring ancient mosaics, working together in squatting positions joining and re-backing mosaic sections from the aspe floor of a church built in the 6th century. There were others, identically attired in large aprons, piecing together another section of mosiacs which appeared to be different in design and age. I asked my host to inquire from the artist about this particular project.

"Cosa sta per restaurare adesso?" she asked (What are you restoring now?). I was told it was part of an old house. "This is the back side of the mosaic," she explained, pointing to the dried mortar. They were restoring it for future exhibit.

I could just imagine what a very close friend of mine, the highly esteemed artist Michele Russo, and his charming wife of more than 60 years, Sally Haley (another true artist of great ability), would have given to be in my shoes just for those few precious hours. Both are admirers of this ancient art and Michele, a renowned painter in oils, has also worked with mosaics. Later, when I told him of my recent visit to the studios of Ravenna, he showed me an example of his own work in mosaics which was hanging in, and lending a further artistic dimension to, his garden.

I told Michele that a group of mosaicists who specialized in restoration, along with others whose work was purely creative, had formed a limited liability company in 1984 to work at restoring mosaics. The group, I was told, has been active not only in restoring the mosaics of Ravenna but also in translating works of contemporary painters into the medium of mosaics. Some of the translations involve the masterpieces of Marc Chagall, Hans Erni, Domenico Cantatore and others.

The art of mosaics is centuries old. The technique involves utilizing small pieces of stone which have been individually cut to fit into a design. Seeing how this was executed gave me a deeper insight into the talents of these artists. Whether the mosaics celebrate the triumph of Christianity, the imperial glory of Rome or the translated works of contemporary painters, they exhibit a unique testimonial to an art and craft which is very much alive today.

When I entered the tomb holding the sarcophagus of Galla Placidia, the Roman empress, the profusion of gold on the mosaics was so characteristic of the Oriental influence. There was beauty in the colors and lightness in the detail. Our host and guide told us that the sarcophagus at one time contained the remains, but that in all probability the empress was buried in Rome where she died in 450 A.D. The sarcophagus was made of Greek marble, and reflected what was described as the pagan style of the time. Other mosaics shown to us included the memorial to Saint Vitale, who was a martyred Roman soldier killed because he professed his Christianity.

———

Before we left Ravenna (and owing to the restrictions of time we had seen only a small part of it) we had dinner at one of the most interesting restaurants on our trip, the Enoteca near Dante's tomb on the Via C. Ricci. The building in which it was located could easily have pre-dated Dante's tomb. The restaurant, once perhaps a single huge, high-ceilinged hall, was divided into giant rooms each decorated with an individualistic wine theme. In one room the ceilings, at least 30 feet high, were supported by bare brick walls to which were attached shelves containing an array of red and white wines.

Our meal was of barbecued and roasted meats of all kinds, a specialty of the region. Trays and trays of beef and turkey and fowl were brought to the table—enough to feed an army of journalists. There were baskets of the traditional "piadina" bread, the size of large pancakes and made simply from wheat flour, salt, baking powder and pork fat, cooked on a hot skillet. It was somewhat similar to pita bread, only a little heavier in texture. Then we had more cappelletti with a cheese filling, cooked in a capon broth. Our dessert included Romagnol ciambella and "zuppa inglese," a kind of trifle made with custard and cordial-soaked biscuits. Our wines included the region's famous Sangiovese and Albana. We were joined by city officials and other local celebrities who treated us with hospitality, Italian style. What more can one ask for? We ate and drank until it was time to leave.

This was the Italy they don't put on travel posters or in brochures; in that Italy you rarely, if ever, get a chance to actually talk to Italians during meals. But here we were at long family-type tables, seated not only with our group but with other

Italians, including city officials, enjoying one of Ravenna's sumptuous evenings of gastronomic pleasure.

Ravenna is situated only a few miles from some of the finest beaches in Italy, beaches that are the most beautiful on the Adriatic Sea. I had been forewarned about the attraction of these beaches, which can only be described by one who possesses the pen of a Byron and the soul of a Dante. I had to satisfy myself only with the brochures handed to us by the tourist bureau in Ravenna in the final minutes of our stay. They stressed the beauty of the beaches such as Milano Marittima, Lido Adriano, Lido di Dante, Lido di Classe and others, all within the Ravenna area. To make our departure even more painful, the brochures featured lithe figures portrayed as typical habitués of these seashores on the Adriatic. It was not mere puffery; we had seen in seven rare days the beautiful people who frequented the restaurants and the plazas, not least of whom were the hosts who had made our visit such a joy and pleasure.

But for now, it was sadly, "ciao" to dear Ravenna, and to Italy. Tomorrow we were homeward bound.

ABOUT THE AUTHOR

Joe Bianco is an award-winning Oregon journalist and author of six books. Among his awards are the Peabody Award for a TV documentary on the 1980 earthquake in Italy. He holds an honorary doctorate from the University of Portland.

He is a passionate student and teacher of Italian cooking. His love of cooking began many years ago, when he was asked to write a cookbook remembering his mother's recipes brought to America from her home, Guardia Lombardy, in the Neapolitan region of Italy. That book, *Cooking Italian*, is distributed nationally and is in its third printing.

He has also taught cooking at schools in Portland, Oregon and held seminars throughout the Pacific Northwest, as well as appearing as a guest cook and lecturer on "love boats."

The family histories of both parents, who come from the same town, go back to the late 15th century. The author's strong attachment to his ancestral roots has resulted in many visits to the native land of his parents. It has also earned for him recognition for his many years of volunteer work with the internationally known Boys Towns of Italy. He was recipient of a Presidential gold medal for this effort.